Little Bit

Little Bit

Anthony Lamb

To order additional copies of this book, contact:
Xlibris Corporation
1-888-795-4274
www.Xlibris.com
Orders@Xlibris.com
63506

Trick pulled around the corner knowing this would be his last drug deal. He had already saved up over a hundred and twenty thousand dollars now all he had to do was deliver his last nine ounces to a would be first time buyer named Carlos.

The tires on the sky blue seventy six Park Avenue made a popping noise as they rolled over the small dirt road leading to Carlos's hang out. Trick was prepared for the worse and the only thing on his mind was leaving for Florida at the end of next week.

Trick exited his car cocking his nine-millimeter and tucking it safely in the small of his back. Knock, knock. Who is it a voice spoke through the other side. It's me Trick. The tall dark skinned young man in his early twenty's said, Hold on just a minute, the voice spoke through the door. There was a short silence then the lock clicked and the door opened. Carlos stood at a counter counting money as Trick stepped in the house.

Well I see you had no problem finding the house the short man spoke with a portarecan descent. No not at all Carlos not at all. Now lets get down to business I have the nine ounces in powder I know I had told you I was going to have it already cooked up for you but time fell short and something came up. Do you have a problem with that Trick said? No not at all not at all Carlos responded.

Trick became very suspicious he always had been particular about doing business with someone he didn't know, it sent him into a paranoid state of mind that would often make him reach for his gun and this time was not exception. Here's the five thousand dollars you requested for your product. Now that the business is out of the way would you like a drink maybe a shot of Pairadess on the rocks or would you prefer Remy Martin himself.

Ha ha ha, Carlos chuckled as he finished his statement-making Trick even more suspicious. No thanks Trick said I think I've had enough it was great doing business with you but I have to run and here is the number of one of my other connections in case you can't get in touch with me next time.

Just then the back door flew open and a tall light skinned young lady in a blue jean skit outfit, red knee high stockings, white Air Force One's, long hair braided into long braids from the front of her head to the back with two red ball braid holders and a mac-10 semi automatic hand gun stood directly in his path.

All right give me the money and the dope the young lady said and don't make this a problem or the cops un never find yo ass. Nobody make a move Carlos looked at Trick, Trick looked back at Carlos, Carlos then pulled out two chrome pearl handle three eighty pistols from his waist area.

The young lady made a turning motion positioning the barrow of the mac-10 on Carlos, when Trick pulled his nine-millimeter from the small of his back. The guns started ta bark. Carlos's first, Carlos managed to spit three bullets from his three eighty's hitting the young lady in the thigh once before the mac-10 rittled his body throwing him across the floor.

The young lady managed to move out the door way in to the house when Trick started to bust at her from behind she tried to run but the bullets ripped through her knee cap and back buy the time she turned around. She didn't really have control of the gun anymore the shots made her body tense and her hands ball up into fists.

Trick tried to duck but it was to late the first bullet hit'em in the stomach causing him to fold over the second bullet grazed his ear causing him to drop his gun under the kitchen table. Staggering through the kitchen the young lady managed to find cover on the side of the stove.

Trick groaned as he reached for his pistol holding on to his stomach with the other hand he could hear the young lady breathing very hard as if she was having a baby and saw that Carlos was already dead laying in a puddle of blood.

The young lady cursed to herself calling Trick to the floor for a last showdown. You'll never leave alive I's going to kill you before I die just like your friend the lady said. Bitch soon as you raise your head from behind that stove I'm going to rip a hole in it the size of your dirty pussy you uh dead bitch still walkin Trick said.

She rolled her eyes gritting her teeth and counted to ten then rose from behind the stove holding the mac-10 with a firm grip only to see Trick on his knees leaning over a chair with both hands on his pistol they both fired at the same time. The girl's bullets missed but Tricks bullet hit its target right in between the eyes. She fell forward slumped over the stove blood ran from her brain like a water fountain.

Trick sat there for a minute thinking about what he had got himself into then gathered up the money and drugs got in his car and left bleeding bad. He made it to the hospitals emergency room opened the car door and fell to the ground. Paramedic doctors, nurses and hospital security surrounded the car but it was too late Trick was dead.

Music blasted through the projects young women danced in the alley ways while local drunks watched in amazement, the nigga's smoked on weed as they sold drugs to the neighborhood junky's, and the kids watched the sky light up every second. It was the Fourth of July and bumper ta bumper traffic, and partying in Barrowhead projects, and also the home of the most notorious drug dealer gangster in the city David Wakefield better known as Trick.

Trick's main girl Little Bit was busy in the kitchen preparing food for the young kids in the hood while niggas & bitch's kept running in and out grabbing somin ta snack on. She stood five seven about uh hundred and eighty pounds with her hair hanging past her shoulders, caramel complexion and uh body that was one of a kind.

No one dared talked to her not eve Tricks other hoes. Everyone knew her and spoke to her but none never even made a pass not even the rival gangs like the Chanel's a all lady gang or the Barrowhead Possies most hated enemy the Lowriders a Latino gang mostly men and a few women.

Face busted in the back door of Little Bits apartment screamin and yellin so loud that she couldn't understand what he was saying. Calm down Face, get control of yaself you look like one of them clams on dat shit right about now, lower your voice and talk clear so I can hear you now what you say Little Bit said.

He dead he got shot in the stomach and lost a lotta blood on the way to the hospital by the time he got there it was to late Face said. NO! No! It can't be dats not true your lying get out my house I hate you. Why! Why! Face I told em not to go alone he wouldn't listen Little Bit said. Go where Little Bit, where tell me and I'll round up the fellas and roll down there ta check things out. He wouldn't tell me.

By now Little Bits face had filled up wit tears her eyes were dark pink but she still managed to throw a ponytail in her hair turn off the stove and grab her keys. Where you going? To the hospital, the police already seized the car they found a gun, five thousand cash, and a quarter bird soft. Damn did you tell anybody yet? No, well don't they'll all wanna come over and get on my nerves and I don't feel like being bothered lets go.

Later on that night Little Bit sat in her room and cried thinking about all the good times her and Trick had together. She thought it was pitiful for her ta be actin like she was but with out him she was nothing just another project ho wit us welfare check. Soon all the payments would fall behind and everything would have ta go back unless she found out where he kept his drugs.

She had a couple of ounces but she knew it wouldn't last even if she hustled day and night with help from other gang member's. The Lexus, Benz, Escalade, Excursion, Hummer, DTS Bentley, twenty-five houses and seven business's scattered all over the city. It would be hard to keep gas ta find everything she thought and if she let anyone in the house she knew that they would probably find it or put a gun to her head.

Mostly everything was in her name but business was slow she had to find the drugs and quick. Little Bit tore the entire apartment up looking for drugs, money and bank receipts. She managed to find six thousand dollars an extra set of keys to the Excursion a phone number, and an envelope with a return address.

Inside the letter read. Dear Little Bit I wanted to tell you face to face about my plans to move ta Florida, but I figured if I wrote you a letter it would be more romantic, my life isn't here I need a change I'll send for you later. Love Trick.

He wasn't even going to tell me he was going to leave without me. She picked up the phone and dialed the number on the small sheet of paper. No one answered she then took the money to her bedroom and stuck it in the top drawer with her panties. Tomorrow I'll go and check this address out she thought to herself.

The next morning Little Bit woke up and looked out her bedroom window only ta see Gutta, Co-Co, and Eleiat standing outside sellin. She raised the window and hollered out what's up yaw hungry? Hell yeah they all said. Well I'll open the door in uh minute just give me time to get downstairs. Ok. Little Bit opened the door Co-Co came in. Where are Eleiat and Gutta Little Bi said? Oh they went to the car ta get some more kill we been getting high all morning and I'm starving. Co-Co said.

Well don't worry girl I'm bout to make some bacon and eggs it'll be done in not time. Gutta came in wit a Mossberg pump followed b Eleiat who carried an A-K 47 assault riffle. "Bitch where the money at? Tricks ass dead and you will be to if you don't come off the cash" Gutta said. "Ah-Ah-Ah" Little-bit and Co-Co said, "shut up bitches before I off you dumb ass hoes what you thought we was going to let you keep all the money? Now where's the cash?" Eleiat said. "Upstairs in my bedroom just take it! Take it all and leave" Lil-Bit said. "You better hope it's enough bitch" Gutta said. "What you lookin at anyway Co-Co? You ain't nothing but a weed head hoe get in the closet bitch so we can take care of our business wit Lil-Bits fine ass" Gutta said. Both girls looked at each other like they knew what was gong on, they where going to rape Lil-Bit and leave her for dead.

Gutta hollered upstairs to Eleiat "Did you get the dough yet? Yeah, well bring it down and don't try an take anything out. How much is it he whispered to Little-Bit and don't try to be smart". It its six thousand dollars. He grabbed the phone cord and rapped it around the doorknob until it was only enough to tie Co-Cos wrist together. "Stop you crazy mothafucka I thought you loved me? Well you was wrong bitch I was just usin you all along now that I got what I want I don't need yo ass no more" Gutta said. Looking in to Little-Bits eyes as she set on the couch in a short nightgown with her legs open just enough to see her sky blue and green lace panties.

Little Bit was no amateur to the game and knew what was ahead for her if she didn't cooperate with Gutta. She had managed to position her butt side ways on the couch enough for Gutta to notice it, running her fingers threw her hair while thinking about Trick made her nipples stand up as she licked her lips and smacked on the little piece of gum she had in her mouth. Eleiat returned downstairs wit the money rapped in a white wife beater. What you want me to do now he said. Go and get the car put the money in the trunk and drive to my house I'll call you later when I'm done wit these bitch's.

Eleiat did as he said and went to the car. Gutta then took the Mossberg and laid it on top of the fifty-two inch screen plasma T.V. He walked back toward the couch where Little Bit was sitting unbuttoning his pants at the same time.

You know you want it bitch he said as he pulled out his growing now suck this dick for daddy. Little Bit grabbed his growing with both hands and took him inside her mouth paying him no attention as she went to work. Gutta cuffed the back of her head with one hand watching in amazement as he pulled the left shoulder of her silk night gown until a firm beautiful titty popped out.

Saliva dripped from her mouth as she looked up into Gutta's eyes only to see them closed it was time for her to except him in her life as if he was her man and she knew it. After this she was sure that he would want to experiment with her beautiful body and explore what she had to offer behind the luxurious nightgown that seemed to barely be left on her body.

Gutta pulled the other shoulder down then told her to slip out of the rest on her own. She did as she was told. He stood there for a second and admired the beautiful peace of work in front of his face. When Little Bit was done she looked up at Gutta and said did you enjoy that, his facial expression changed to curious he always had wondered what was on her mind and started thinking to himself she must just be a freak of nature.

She continued to stare at him pushing her hand down her panties and fondling her breast with her other hand. He stepped closer only to see her pull her legs up high in the air then grab the seat of her panties rapping them around her wrist exposing her soaking wet vagina. Gutta fell to his knees wrapped up in emotions, little Bit grabbed the back of his neck pulling him close burying his face in between her breast.

Gutta then entered her slowly thinking that maybe it was something hears a love that she might have before and never knew. Little Bit tilted her head back moaning and moving her body back and forth up against his till she felt him shaking in between her legs that's when she knew she had to pretend that she was cumming to. After it was over she watched him get dressed grab his Mossberg and turn and say it's best you keep your mouth shut if you know what's best for you then walked out the door. Co-Co and Little Bit both knew what that meant if he thought the cops were on to him he'd come back and kill both of dim.

Untie me! Untie me! Please I didn't know they were planning to rob you bit Co-Co said. I know Bit said as she untied Co-Co. What did the do to you girl I'll kill both of dim if they hurt you in any way. I'm all right it's nothing a girl like me can't handle. You sure? Yeah I'm sue forget about it for now I have other things on my mind. Like what Co-Co said. Like how I'm going to hold my own out here how I'm going to keep Tricks ship runnin like he did dats what up you feelin me bitch. Yeah, Yeah I'm definitely feelin you haw can I help. Well I gotta couple ounces left and I need some help getting rid of this shit any suggestions.

First let me call my people and second I don't think it's good to try and do business in Barrowhead right now we both know all dim niggas Trick dealt with is scandals and uh rob yo ass quick specially since he's dead, third I gotta little bit uh money saved up too but it's over m house twenty miles from here in Watersdell, but if you can get me there I'll be more than happy to give it to you Co-Co said. Thanks Little Bit said I'll get dressed then we can leave.

Little Bit and Co-Co jumped in the Lexus and dipped. Little Bit was a fast driver wit a I don't give a fuck attitude towards other traffic. She told Co-Co people would always stare at her cuz of the way she drove and blew at dumb ass niggas that couldn't drive a lick. Co-Co laughed then pumped the system loud as UGK's beats bumped through two fifteens in the insulated trunk.

Little Bit was upset but couldn't help boppin her head along with Co-Co to the music. I gotta ditch the lex and pick up the Excursion in storage cuz dim niggas a probably be looking for us in the lex when they run out of money thinking dat I got some more stashed some where she said. Good get rid of this bitch din I'd rather ride twenty fours over twenties any day.

The royal blue excursion pulled around the corner on Co-Co's peoples street Little Bit drove kinda slow cuz she didn't know to much about this hood and Co-Co didn't know the address ta make matters even worse. Dats it! Dats it right there Co-Co said. Where? On your side bit the green house wit light green trim. Oh I see it can I pull in the drive. Yeah it's ok.

Girl you got me over here wit all these niggas and I ain't even got my heat on me. Its cool girl its cool dats my cousin Vinnie standin on the porch he got heat if its uh problem, dim other niggas his homie's dey cool. His main man Duke ain't around but I need to see his fine ass I ain't fucked dat nigga in uh whole year, anyway dat nigga standin on the sidewalk over there dats booner he a small time weight man wit uh lotta connections and dim two niggas standing beside em names are Eric and Harry.

Eric got some pretty ass blue eyes and harry gotta big ass dick ta be uh white boy. Girl you show do know a lot about dess niggas. Well I been knowing em since I was thirteen and they all some freaks we used ta play hid go get it in the back yard. Oh Oh yeah and that last one the one standing behind us across the street wit his head down dats Baby he da one taught me how ta make money sellin at the corner store.

Dat nigga smacked out now though he started fuckin wit da product getting high on the d-l to the product exposed his ass damn dat shit got the best of my nigga. Everybody steal love his ass though mmmm I see you gotta enough stories to right a book or maybe even a dictionary feel me. Little bit went on talking as Co-Co jumped ot the SUV.

What up cuz and what's up wit dat boppa you rollin wit she up for the choosin cuz ya cousin lookin for a lady Vinnie said. Nigga don't try and give my girl no lame ass line like dat she ain't lookin for any young ass nigga dat can't keep his pant up on his ass Co-Co said. Dats fucked up cuz dats fucked up. It's of Co-Co little bit said de cool how old is you anyway Vinnie?

I'm sixteen I will be seventeen pretty soon though. How long you been sellin? Almost three years Vinnie said mmmm you ever drove an escalade on twomps little bit said. Tryin to tease with the young boy you mean a big boy truck he said yeah da kind you can watch TV in an pull pretty bitchs wit.

All right quit flirting wit my friend Vinnie Co-Co said. I gotta little problem what, what is it cuz he said. Well me and little bit need ta make some money fast real fast. How much? Like twenty thousand, cuz now dats a pretty big peace of change. I know but if I get the work you think you and the fellas can push it. Fa show anything for the lovely lady you think maybe you can hook me up. I doubt it but I will make sure I tell her Co-Co said. Just call me when you ready Vinnie said.

Back in the SUV little bit sat patiently waiting on Co-Co when her cell phone rang.

Hello

Bit what's up I heard about what happened where you at. Face calm down I'm in Watersdell wit Co-Co—handling some business she said but I will hit you up soon as we get back to the city she said alright he replied. Little bit was hangin p the phone as Co-Co climbed back in the SUV humming and bobbin her head to a fifty-cent tune in her head.

Girl guess what my little cousin gotta crush on you she said, seriously yeah but fuck dat he said if we come u wit the work he can get it off now take me to my house so I can pick up these ends. How much bit said, close to three thousand twenty seven hundred to be exact.

On the ay to Watersdell the girls conversated and talked about everything Little Bit had told face she was already in Watersdell on the phone and that was a straight out lie she had more important things on her mind at the time. Does your cuz have a girlfriend bit said. Yeah Co-co said. He's kinda cute I'm thinking bout takin him out ta dinner later on. You know what come ta think about it I forgot to ask Vinnie where Duke was. Don't worry girl we gone hook up wit dim niggas later.

Bitch can't you see I'm tryin ta get off the e-way move yo blind ass out the way bit said blowing the horn. Co-co sat in the passenger seat giving the lady and her family the finger. I can just imagine what the bitch is thinking Co-co said, probably how stupid her ass look in front of her family dumb bitch bit said.

The sun reflected off the twenty inch chrome rims as little-bit hugged the block turning corners an pillin out from lights as if she was playing a video game. Almost there hang a right and park this bitch on the corner, damn girl you show be wiping this bitch for it ta be as big as it is though Co-co said. Experience girl, experience bit said, back in a minute a minute co-co said. Co-co went in the house while little bit sat in the truck and thought about how life was going to be without Trick there to comfort her. Co-co returned to the truck with the cash just as Clyde was pulling up in Tricks dark brown Cadillac DTS.

What's up Clyde she said. Hi you doing miss thang I ain't expect to see you wit Tricks girl tell her I said hi and that she can get the car back anytime she need it any way I just stopped through ta see if . . . ta see if what nigga. The last time you were over here all you did was sit and watch TV. all day you always need a favor, go to the store, pick up my clothes from the cleaners, fix me something ta eat, wash my back I mean you handle yo business and all but don't you know how to treat a lady, comfort a bitch, eat a hoe out or something.

Damn what you on girl the only reason I do you ass like that is cuz you always-high staring at a nigga I thought you wanted to get out and explore the city and shit but I see now all you want to do is sit up in the house and fuck all day, excuse me for trying ta look out for yo ass girl Clyde said smirking.

Oh you think its funny huh, what's up Clyde little bit said as she turned down the music think you can hook a girl up? Anything for my niggas girl what you need he said. I'm trying to get nine of um, but we only hot half the money see I need twenty thousand dollars by the end of this month to pay all the bills she said. I understand little bit Clyde said cutting in on her as if he could take care of everything, she liked that since of power her man had on people

Don't worry I" try to look out for you the best I can and don't worry about the payment on the D.T. S. I'll take care of that and the money you and Co-co got ya'll can keep I'm a throw you a eighthie for free but don't go back to Barrowhead dim niggas over there wildin out in the streets so stay out the way when things calm down I'll let you guys know.

Clyde parked the car popped the trunk and got out he moved a couple things around then pulled out a black gym bag, he then walked over to the girls pulled open the back door and set the bag on the floor. Be careful he said waving his hand on the way back to the car. OK we a holla Co-co said as little bit sped off. Girl it looks like you in luck after all and wit dat nigga on yo team you sure ta come up. Who you think be payin my rent every month? Him dats who Co-co said.

I guess I'm lucky to have a girl like you on my team little bit said. You show is girl, you show is. Little-bit finally pulled the big SUV in to a McDonalds parking lot and parked both girls got out and walked towards the entrance. Look Co-co said there's one of them Chanel girls getting out of that car over there bit said. Don't worry girl she probably won't even notice us and anyway if she does I'll kick her little skinny ass ugly bitch se know better that ta be over this way anyway Co-co said.

The girls walked in the restaurant and stood in line waiting for the cashier to take their orders. Co-co I'm going to the rest room and when she comes in if she gives you any trouble I'll sneak up and mop her ass bit said. Word Co-co replied. Little-bit walked in the bathroom looking around for some kind of disinfectant spray to blind the Chanel girl if she gave Co-co any problem.

Under the sink she found a bottle of Lysol then stuffed it in her purse. The toilet mad a flushing sound then another flushing sound when all of a sudden the door flung open and a short young lady exited the stall walking towards the vanity bar she reached over turning the water on her hands while she rubbed them together not paying little bit any attention.

Bitch hurry yo ass up she said, mmmm little bit thought to herself I wonder who's she talking to when the other door swung open little-bit quickly put her and on the spray bottle hidden in her purse as she saw Yo-yo the reputed leader of the Chanels exit the urinal. Bitch what you lookin at yo man dead now you want to fight Yo-yo said.

What little bit said amazed the girl even said something that ignorant, first of all I don't know you just know of you second of all I ain't nobody's bitch, bitch. Slowly pulling the spray bottle from her purse she doused Yo-yo dead in the eyes sending her in to a wild spinning motion when the short girl decided to crack her in the jaw bit dropped the spray bottle on the floor charging the shorter lady ripping the chains from her neck smacking and pulling hair at the same time.

Little bit was getting the best of the shorter girl when she tripped over Yo-yo leg and fell to her stomach the shorter lady then jumped on bits back pulling her hair banging her head into the cement floor. Yo-yo stumbled trying to get back to her feet before little bit grabbed her leg pulling her back down. She noticed a leather casing wrapped around Yo-yo's leg with a Velcro strap, she pulled on the case till it came loose from her leg when she noticed it was a mini pocketknife.

Pulling the case toward her opening it at the same time she managed to maneuver her body sideways now all she had to do was find a good place to stick her without thinking she drew the knife from her side swinging hard as she could in seconds the girl dropped to the floor not moving. Little bit then got up and tied Yo-yo's wrist together with her purse strap shoving wads of toilet paper into her mouth then dragging her to the door she looked back and noticed the but of a knife hanging out the short girls neck and decided to leave them both and run out the back door hoping no one noticed her when she came in.

When she got back to the truck she called Co-co on her cell phone, Hello who is dis Co-co screamed in to the phone trying to attract the Chanel girls attention. Girl hurry up she said. Who is this? It's me bit. What you whispering for girl where you at anyway? I'm in da truck bout ta leave yo ass if you don't hurry up. How you end up out there? Don't worry bout dat and huh I'll tell you when you get here.

Alright I'm on my way co-co picked up the bags looked at ol girl and walked out the door switchin her hips. What's up? What's up is dim bitch's tried to jump my ass in the bathroom. For real huh knew huh shoulda beat dat bitch's as damn!

And dat ain't the only thing I end up having ta kill one of dim bitches plus tie Yo-yo's ass up. Yo-yo dat bitch was in there to hell naw girl dis shit crazy you know dat shit gone be on the news tonight. I know, I know, I gotta thing of something, maybe I can wait and see what happens later on the news you know see if they have any suspects.

Back in Barrowhead face was busy dealing trying ta make ends meat little one one of the younger members had been buyin work off him all day. What up young Shorty I see you out hear doing yo thang you got protection face said? Hell Yeah. What you thought uh bitch ain't going to protect her grissol you no I got my pistol cocked and ready for whatever. Shit been stankin every since Trick died that's why I'm itching to pop a fool Little One said. Shit girl you talking like a real O.G. got me convinced you ever been to fool school. He said fool school nigga what the fuck is that you on that shit again ain't you? You quit smoking so damn much weed all the time she said. Naw Little One I'm thinking about riding down on them niggas that shot Trick you know blowing up in they spot getting dirty. Yeah that sound good I'm wit it hit me up when you ready 911 she said.

Back at Vinnie's Duke had just pulled up in a black drop top mustang fresh off the lot. Shake a leg nigga he said we got a date you know Treese gone kick yo ass and mine to if you don't show up wit me as planned. Nigga where you get off thinking she runs shit anyway? I'm about to drop that bitch in a minute if she don't straighten her act y'all got that bitch thinking she run shit and don't sell a lick of dope. All she do is run her mouth all fuckin day Vinnie said.

She is playing you! Duke said anyway cuz she asked about yo today Vinnie said. Who co-co Duke said. Yeah she came over wit some badass bitch name Lil-Bit. They want me to get some work off for them Vinnie said. They payin Duke said?. Naw but its a lot Vinnie said. Man its cool you know I will help my nigga out. Anyway we goin bowlin on Ree-Ree she got some extra tickets and took it upon herself to invite you and Treese Duke said.

Lets get a room tonight just you and me and chill out said Little-Bit said to Co-Co, okay whatever is cool wit you is cool wit me. Damn I almost forgot to go check this address I need to see who stays there mmmm . . . let me see it's in here somewhere. Oh here it is you know where 1475 Bell Street is? Lil-Bit said. Bell Street uh yeah I do no where Bell Street is Co-Co said well get me there Lil-Bit said. Okay Co-Co said. Ring Ring Ring Ring yeah who dat is Bit said. Its me Face you still got that work? Yeah she said. Well I uh give you two thousand right now for that shit he said

Mmmm . . . okay meet me at the Bestwestern in a hour she said, what's the room number? He said. I don't gotta room yet so just call me in forty-five minutes and I will and I will let you know she said. All right I uh be waiting he said and hung up the phone. This the street right here Lil-Bit turn, ten oh two three ten oh two two five ok we going the right way, what that nigga talking about Co-Co said. He wanna get that work girl and I got it he going to meet us at the tellie maybe we can talk him out of it my pussy get hot at the smell of money, plus I no he probably wanna buy some of his tuna cat anyway Lil-Bit said.

Girl you crazy I do need some dick Co-Co said girl we then passed the house talking shit Lil-Bit said. What's so funny I ain't trying to offend you but every since yo man died you been foot loose and fancy free ha ha ha Co-Co said. I know I get like that when I'm down sex fuckin and romance makes me feel better though Llil-Bit said. I feel you girl you know I'm a lot like that to Co-Co said.

Back in Barrowhead Face stood on the corner waiting for Lil-Bit to call, a car pulled up with four Latino men inside. Hey you got some work the driver yelled, how much Face said as all three passengers pulled out their weapons. Face quickly turned trying to make a run for it when the first bullet rang out echoing threw the projects then crashing into the pavement. One after another bullets started to spray tearing holes into Faces back then exiting threw his chest.

As he fell to the pavement the car swerved as the driver struggled to regain control screeching threw the street t over fifty miles per hour. Disappearing in a cloud of smoke the local women and children quickly gathered around the body as blood seeped threw wounds leaking on the pavement.

Yo-Yo sat locked in a small interrogation room at the public station waiting for the detectives to figure out what they were going to charge her with. While she thought of a way to kill Lil-Bit for what she had done to her friend Chocolate she knew in her mind that she was in assent but had to convince the detectives she was.

The detective entered the room and sat directly across from Yo-Yo. Miss winters I'm sorry to have incarcerate you but us detectives must interrogate every one at the scene before letting them walk its just routine procedures you are free to go now and have a nice day. Yo-Yo quickly left the room determined to find Lil-Bit for what she had done. On the way out the police station she noticed a familiar face on the front page of the newspaper she inserted a quarter and took one copy on the way out. I'm gone do that bitch like you Yo-Yo thought as she stared at Tricks photo on the front page.

Oh shit she said drawing attention to herself as she read the article involving Claireece a childhood friend of hers and once a member of the Chanels in the early days.

Mmmm . . . says right here that the police suspect foul play was involved suspect that a drug deal went sour. Case closed all suspects dead . . . Carlos Valdess, Claireece Thomas, and David Wakefield, bitch done got my girl knocked off to. Barrowhead is goin to pay now. Yo-Yo was starting to snap, loosing composure and break down. The deaths of her two friends was beginning to take a toll she needed revenge but first she had to call Newnie to pick her up.

Duke pulled up to Re-Res house where her and Treese were waiting on the front porch. Come on y'all Duke said, I'm coming don't be rushing us boy Re-Re said. Treese came around to the passenger side where Vinnie was sitting "Ain't you going to get in the back wit me" she said? Hell naw I don't feel like being cooped up in that little ass back seat with the likes of you Vinnie said. I see so you want to be a smart ass tonight huh, well keep it up you wont be getting any of this pussy Mr. All of that Treese said.

Duke sat in the drivers seat talking to Re-Re who was standing right at the door teasing him. This is such a nice ride I wanna drive it she said. Get yo smart-ass in the car and quit stunting for yo girl Vinnie said. She ain't paying me no attention don't you see her over there playing with the wheel? Look like the only on her mind tonight is driving Treese said, Vinnie looked over his shoulder admiring the fresh interior while glancing into Dukes and Re-Res eyes noticing how much their moods had changed. He then quickly turned back to Treese and who you think wear the pants in this here relationship anyway Miss Thang Vinnie said.

Me of course Treese stated with her hands on her hips. Well I'm glad you've helped me see the light Vinnie rolled his eyes as he motioned for her to get in. Both girl piled in the back seat as they drove off. Lil-Bit pulled up in the drive way curiously looking at the house she started to think maybe it was another women in Tricks life and maybe she was out of place sitting in her drive way. Maybe we should go little bit said I'm not feeling right about this whole thing anymore.

Look girl if you drove all the way out here and don't wanna go in that's on you I'm just the passenger co-co said. I'll just knock first before I go stuffing keys into the locks you know some one else could stay here little bit said stepping out the SUV.

OK little bit I'll just wait in the truck co-co said. Little bit gave a couple taps on the door she looked into the window as if she was casing the house out to be burglarized. She didn't see anyone so she knocked a couple more times even louder still no one came so she decided to start trying the keys.

First she accidently tried slipping the Excursion key into the licked door. Ooops she said nervously fumbling while moving the keys around in her fingers. OK maybe this one, no ok lets try this one neither of the keys matched. Damn she said wait a minute what am I so nervous for I'm Tricks girl she thought to herself calm down and take your time she gasped.

OK I'll try this one right here she thought placing the key into the lock "it fits" she gently turned the key sideways releasing the lock from the exterior of the wall then slowly started to twist the door knob. She turned and waved at co-co letting her know it was cool then walked into the house.

The layout on this house is beautiful co-co said walking up behind little bit rushing as if she was in a hurry to see the rest of the house. Wait a minute co-co we don't know is anyone stays here so take it easy little bit said. Looking at the mail on the dining room table mmmm David Wakefield, David Wakefield, Dave Wakefield, well I guess it's ok trick musta stayed here or just used this spot to make deals but we'll have to search top to bottom just to make sure little bit said.

The girls quickly started to search the beautiful house opening closets ram shacking drawers and lifting mattresses. I think we can definitely say this was one of tricks houses you didn't know about co-co said. I know but not one he renovated little bit said looking at the pictures on the master bedroom wall remembering how much she loved art back in high school.

I think I'll take one of these pictures with me to keep for myself pulling the frame from the wall, oh my god look co-co it's a safe hidden behind the picture frame she said. I see co-co said. I know it's some money in there co-co and I bet it's probably a lot little bit said. Maybe we can find something in the basement to get it open co-co said. I hope so lets go check it out little bit said.

The girls made their way through the house down to the basement they were surprised by the set up fully furnished big screen television mini kitchen bathroom and laundry area. This layout is bangin more than any other hotel I've been to little bit maybe we can get some time to ourselves out here after we've finished safe cracking. Yeah I'm down with that my kitty's ready for a layover and your cousin can be the on to do it.

Look another safe, mmmm that's odd why would Trick keep two safes in one house and not let me know anything about it. You know how men are bit they never let someone they love know everything. Yeah look what I found though holdin up a small butane torch. We can bust our way in with this thing for sure bit said. OK I think we should stay with this one right here co-co said.

I don't give uh fuck where we start long as we crack dis bitch so I can get some dick tonight. The started to burn the door of the safe watching as the metal started to melt the girls started to cheer when they saw the first lock fall patiently waiting for the last one.

The safe door fell to the floor as the girls waited for the smoke to clear so they could see what was inside. That sure does look like a lot of money and drugs co-co said as little bit grabbed all the content out and set them on the table. Two keys and sixty thousand dollars sat in front of the girls as bit blazed up the blunt. Now that what I'm talkin bout girl wit dis shit right here I'm on you hear me girl on fuck crackin the other on tonight I'm ready to get fucked how bout it.

Mmmm I don't know bit maybe you should, naw first I gotta cop another safe for dis shit to go in then I'll pop the other one but right now I'm gonna call Face and see what's up.

Face laid in the hospital bed unconscious while the doctors and nursed worked to save his life. Ring, ring get that phone out of here one of the doctors said, a nurse quickly searched through Faces clothes to find the phone she then quietly walked out the operating room leading to the hall where faces mom was sitting. Excuse me mam your son's phone. Thank you the lady said as she answered the line. Hello, Face.

This isn't face this is his mom he's on the operating table he's been shot several times in the chest who am I speaking with anyway. This is little bit I'm sorry to hear that what hospital is he in? Zion, I'll be right there mam, little bit hung up the phone. What, Face got shot he's in critical condition we gotta go down to Zion and see what the deal is help me hide this stuff so we can go ok.

Stop bitch don't you see me standing right here Yo-Yo screamed to Nennie. Scoot over I'm driving look at this shit yo-yo passed Nennie the paper as she climbed in the driver seat. What's this, read it, I'm bout sick chocolates dead, Claireece is dead, and dat bitch little bit running around here like miss goodie two shoes.

Nennie knew how yo-yo was when she was upset so she fired up a blunt and passed it to her to any plans. Not yet but I'm thinking take me to the house so I can strap up. Duke pulled in to the bowling alley and parked. Come on guys we're going to have a nice time tonight Re-re said. Man I ain't feeling this Vinnie first she wanna make plans without letting me know then she wants to act like bowling is fun, we could a went to the all night flite and sold out and got drunk, dis bitch trippin.

What did you say speak up I said I have tickets for drink to now you want me to get drunk and start acting a fool. Hell naw you don't so treat me nice and I'll make it up to you promise. Hey take me inside so I can get my drink on Treese said. Vinnie liked like he was going to throw up just looking at her he knew she was going to show out and didn't really want to have to beat her ass but the urge was slowly growing beneath his skin.

Shut up, make me square ass nigga you know what you only act like this when you get around duke Vinnie, cut her off bitch don't try and get loud tonight or I uh beat yo ass in front of yo girl. Tresse started crying leaning on Re-re's shoulder he called m a bitch in front of you guys and said he would beat my ass if I got smart with him tonight. Don't worry girl I'll make sure he doesn't lay a finger on you ok.

The girls started walking toward the bowling alley while duke and Vinnie stood by the ca smoking a blunt. Man what's up you trying to holla at my cousin tonight or what. Why. Because I told you I'm trying to get with little bit. I mean I don't really give a fuck ma nigga what ever you wanna do ok. Let's just go in here and play it cool for a while then act like we got something important to do, yeah sounds like a good plan.

When the guys got inside the girls had already got shoes and found lane to bow in. You tow look excited ya'll ready to get ya'll ass kicked by the balled wit pro bowling patencal duke said. Yeah right I thought it was going to be boy girl though Treese said smiling at Vinnie trying to win his live back.

Oh so you switching sides now hoe Re-re said. They all laughed as Re-re punched up the names on the computed consol looks like your first Vinnie she said pointing to the balls. Don't laugh at me cuz I can't bowl a lick Vinnie said grabbing the ball with both hands slipping across the floor as he got prepared to throw the ball.

Three pins that's not bad for a beginner now it's my turn but I promise I wont embarrass you guys. Re-re threw the ball knocking every pin down clearing the lane strike Duke yelled as Re-re ran to his arms kissing his lips. Looks like it's your turn Duke soon as you and Re-re get finish making love over there Treese said. Oh ok here I come let me go bay so I can show these clowns the deal Duke said.

Little bit pulled in the hospital parking lot and parked as her and co-co rushed to the emergency entrance. Excuse me lady but we're looking for some guy that got shot tonight co-co said. Well do you girls have a name the nurse said. Both girls liked at each other realizing neither of them knew Face's real name. we just called his cell phone and found out he was down here little bit said.

So I take it ya'll don't know his name. Not exactly just his nickname co-co said. Witch is, Face little bit said. Ok give me a second while I call around and see if I can dind out what's going on girls. Co-co and little bit took a seat in the waiting room as the nurse called down to surgery, ring ring, yes I have two young lad's over here in emergency asking about a gunshot victim do you guys know anything about it.

Yes but only the family is aloud back here at his time, but I can send the mother down to fill them in on any activity their curious about. Fine I'll let them know bye. Lady's the nurse down in surgery said no one's aloud back there except family members but she's going to send the mother out to see you guys. Great thanks a lot for everything we'll just wait for his mom to come out little bit said.

Damn I'm glad to be home Nnnie them fuckin coppers tried to give me the third degree you know them bitches thought I had killed chocolate Yo-yo said. What Nennie said. Yeah talkin bout they gonna lick me up and throw away the key if I don't start confessing. How, dats what I said how I'm gonna confess to somthin I ain't do. For real hell naw girl dats fucked up Nennie said.

Well you see where a bitch at now my mouth always getting me out us shit girl ta be for real I don't think dey could a licked me up even if I did do it. Dats what I'm talkin bout a crazy ass bitch dat can get away wit anything I'm feelin dat shit all the way Yo-yo Nennie said.

Yo-yo loaded up her two three eighty's and stuffed um in her purse then strapped her 25 on her right ankle let me see your box cutter Nennie. Nennie reached in her pocket to retrieve the box cutter and handed it to Yo-yo who then stuck it down her panties now I'm ready she said. Where you gone start at? I don't know maybe coast the outskirts of Barrowhead see if we can catch anybody slippin you know the usual shit we do when I'm lookin to take somebody out.

Yeah, good game Treese day was talkin shit all the way to the end but we still came out on top Vinnie said. We gotta go re-re Duke said. No we gotta another game to play I already paid Re-re said. I know but me and Vinnie gotta move ta make I promise I'll make it up ta you later though Duke said. Aw, why didn't you tell me earlier Vinnie now I'm all wet for nothing Treese said. I just found out myself Vinnie said. Well I don't mean to be rude but we gotta go now Duke said.

Damn ok let me take these shoes back and I'll be ready Re-re said. Meet us in the car lady luck and putta move on it Duke said Treese, Duke and Vinnie walked toward the entrance as Re-re went to return the shoes.

Face's mother walked through the emergency doors leading to the waiting area she didn't know what the girls looked like so she stopped at the desk and asked the nurse to escort her in finding them. Hi there lady's now witch one of you pretty girls name is little bit she said. That would be me mam we rushed right down here is there anything we can do to help?

Not right now all I can do is hope the doctors are doing all they can do in the operating room but I still haven't heard anything. I hope hi's all right we all grew up over in Barrowhead together and we already lost one of our friends this week and don't wanna lose another co-co said.

Oh I'm sorry to hear about that girls it's sad to know there's some mad man out there on the streets trying to kill people and all us women can do is sit here and suffer Faces mom said. I haven't even had time to plan funeral arrangements yet I've been so busy trying to catch up on my bills everything just happen so quick but tomorrow morning I'm going to call and get every thing situated little bit said.

Duke dropped the girls off at home both him and Vinnie had been waiting most of the night to get rid of them so they could try and contact co-co and little bit. Now with them out the way they could do exactly that man, how you plan on getting in contact wit dim anyway its late as fuck and they probably in the bed anyway Duke said. I'm just gone call my cousin's cell phone let it ring a couple times if she don't answer fuck it then.

Vinnie said man I hope she do answer cuz I'm u feel like a big ass dummy if she don't for letting Re-re down. Don't sweat it she'll answer, Vinnie started dialing the digits trying to calm Duke. At the same time the pone rang once before co-co picked it up and said hello what's up cuz where you at Vinnie said? I'm at the hospital right now seeing about a friend of mine she said tapping on little bits leg whispering it's Vinnie pointing at the phone.

She continued to talk as little bit put her ear against the receiver Face's mom just sat there staring at them wondering what was so important about the person on the other end that couldn't wait. So what's up dats why you ain't call me back Vinnie said. Yeah co-co said quickly putting her hand over the phone then asking little bit what to do next.

Tell him to meet us at Tricks house so I can give him the work bit said. But meet us at 1475 Bell Street in half an hour Co-co said. All right cuz I'm a have Duke bring me over since we're already out riding Vinnie said. That's fine with me let me speak to him anyway she said. What's up Duke said. You I ain't seen you in so long I just wanted to say hi and see how you were doing but we can talk more when you guys get to the house stop and pick up a box of blunts so we can smoke for old time sake co-co said.

Yeah I a do dat for you girl here go you cousin Duke said. Vinnie got back on the phone, all right we a holla at ya'll in uh minute he said then hung up the phone. Co-co and little bit got up and danced around the waiting room cheering each other on we gotta go no time to waste sorry mam tell Face we love him we'll stop by tomorrow to check on him bit said. Don't worry yourself girls.

I'm sure he'll be alright you two just make sure you guys enjoy yourselves tonight wherever your going she said. Both girls trotted out the emergency exit racing to the SUV. He don't even know I'm gonna give him some tonight little bit said. Nope he just thinks he comin to pick some dope up and maybe smoke a blunt or two co-co said.

Yo-yo and Nennie rode through Barrowhead looking for little bit most of the night Nennie could tell Yo-yo was frustrated again by the look in her eyes something had to come up she thought but it never did all the two lady's ever accomplished was to get high and drunk before Yo-yo finally decided to turn in for the night. Don't worry girl we gonna find dim bitches before its over and I put that on chocolate nennie said.

Duke and Vinnie sat on Bell street waiting for co-co and little bit to show up man dats what I'm saying day stood us up now I'm gonna have to call Re-re and keep hangin up until she answers the phone Duke said. Man chill out they a be here in a minute there they go right there see I told you ha-ha you was bout to have a fit come on lets meet um at bits SUV wait til you see her you gonna flip Vinnie said.

I bet she ain't even fine nigga Duke said. What's up girl I see you put on a couple pounds since the last time I seen you Duke said, aw I know you ain't trying ta say I'm fat now nigga co-co said. Hell naw girl just think in all the right places he said. Hey Vinnie sorry we were late I know you two probably been waiting out here for a minute but I didn't realize it would take us so long to get here bit said.

That's all right its not really that big of a deal I'm just happy to see you Vinnie said. Well come on lets go in you get the blunts cuz I'm ready to smoke bit said. Yeah we picked dum up on the way like co-co said he replied. Good you know how to roll or you want me to roll it she said. It don't really make a difference to me shit I can't complain I'm smoking for free anyway so I guess I could roll it he said.

Maybe if you guys got time but said as co-co and duke walked up I can cook something ta eat to. Na'll dats all right I done had enough of your cookin to last me a whole lifetime. I'll do the cooking tonight you just take care of the business part ok co-co said laughing. Ok I got it girl bit said, you two enjoying yourselves Duke said. Who co-co said you and Vinnie's rude asses.

Ya'll got me standing around and ain't even introduced me to your friend he said. Oh bit this my nigga Duke, Duke this little bit Vinnie said. Hi Duke I've heard so much about you bit said. Good or bad duke said? Good definitely if it was bad I woulda been sure to let you know she said. Thanks now dats nice to know Duke said, you got that blunt rolled yet cuz co-co said. Yeah Vinnie said, well give it here so I can fire it up she said.

Huh he said, co-co lit the blunt then took a real big hit holding her breath until she started to choke as she fell over on duke's lap purposely trying to gain his undivided attention and hopefully win a chance to get in his pants laughing she pulled her head up looking at little bit. What the matter with you girl you all right bit said. Yeah she said passing Duke the weed. Na'll fuck dat give me a gun you know how we use ta do it in Watersdell he said. All right sit up straight so I can get on top of you I wouldn't want you to lose any smoke.

And I end up being the only one around here high she said laughing. Vinnie you gonna give me a gun to when its my turn to hit it bit said. Yeah he said Damn girl dats some fire ass weed where ya'll get that shit from Duke said. Been had it I coped it over in Barrowhead off them lame ass niggas dat stuck my girl up co-co said.

Vinnie took the weed from co-co and look deep into little bits eyes he could tell she was hurt about what had happen but still was trying to have a nice time. Damn girl somebody as sexy as you seem like a nigga would be ready to kill a nigga just ta get a conversation out of you Vinnie said. Thanks, I'm glad to hear that from somebody like you she said. What you mean he said. I don't know I'm just the type of girl that's always liked to be around my man and now since he's gone it's kinda lonely she said.

Well you can always hang out with us little bit Vinnie said giving her a shotgun lets go in the kitchen and play some cards while I cook us something ta eat co-co said. Ok boys. Everyone went in the kitchen and played cards while co-co cooked fried chicken French fries and a big pitcher of kool-aid.

I'll be right back I have to run upstairs and get that work so you can cook it up then I'll come back down so me and co-co can finish whoopin you and duke in another game of spades little bit said. Great but can you show me where the restroom is he said. Yeah follow me little bit said Vinnie and little bit went upstairs why co-co finished cooking the last peace of chicken you want some bread on your plate duke co-co said?

For sure hook it up girl I'm hungry as fuck he said. Back upstairs little bit separated the drugs as Vinnie came out the bathroom she knew she wanted to try and get at Vinnie but didn't wanna seem like she was being a hoe but at the same time she still needed the attention that only a man could give her. She closed the bedroom door and licked it quickly getting undressed and calling Vinnie's name at the same time.

She knew he would stop and come back towards the room so she ran back towards the bedroom door unlocking it if he tried to bust in while she was getting dressed it wouldn't be like she was trying to be a hoe but at the same time she could expose herself showing him her beautiful body he talked so much about earlier then maybe he would come in and try to seduce her she thought quickly pulling a short night gown over her head to cover all those private places she craved so much for him to explore.

Where you at girl I hear you calling me Vinnie said. Little bit raced to the door cracking it just a little I'm in here I'll be ready in a second she said. Vinnie peeked around the corner just as she hoped he would she went on acting like she was looking for something not paying attention to the cracked door just over her shoulder as Vinnie watched in amazement it was like she could actually hear him breathing outside the door as she leaned forward on the bed looking underneath it exploring the hairless cunt as the tip of her outer vagina lip hung down from between her naked ass cheeks.

She then grabbed the panties she had just took off and started sliding them over her toes and ankles as she stood up and slowly pulled them over her thick thighs Vinnie pulled his head away from the door. She walked toward the closet reaching for a pair of Tricks pajama bottoms he watched as she stood in the closet doorway getting dressed why she had the pajamas all the way on she then lifted the night gown above her breast slowly unsnapping her bra as she turned toward the bedroom door the bra fell to the floor as she cuffed her breast looking in the mirror she let the night gown fall as she started to pin her hair up in a ponytail then wrapping the sides in a scarf.

Vinnie you can come in and sit on my bed while I finish straitening up she said Vinnie stepped in the room acting like he hadn't seen a thing. Here's the work over here by me you can take it downstairs if you want I'll be down in a minute little bit said. Vinnie got up off the bed walking toward the dresser when little bit purposefully stepped in his path brushing up against him rubbing her butt and shoulder against his body he stopped in his tracks to notice her turn toward him placing one hand on the upper of his arm saying excuse me he looked like he had just seen a ghost as she released her hand from his arm.

Then slowly rubbing it across his chest I thought you were still sitting on the bed waitin on me to finish up she said handing him the tightly wrapped key of cocaine. No I, she quickly cut him off by kissing him dead in the mouth dropping the key from his hand her responded by pushing her back against the dresser as she struggled to climb on top we gotta stop what f someone catches us Vinnie said nothing as he helped her on to the dresser.

She struggled to gain control wrapping her head around his neck whispering in his ear panting. Just let me take my pajamas off Vinnie continued to ignore her as she worked her fingers unbuckling his shorts as fast as possible once his shorts were down she could see him standing in front of her fully erect he reached and grabbed at one loose fitting pajamas pulling and tugging them until they were down just up under her butt.

He slowly threw himself inside of her only to fill her soft insides rubbing against his penis. Vinnie quickly fulfilled his sexual fantasy with in the next five minutes assuring little bit she still had what it takes to satisfy a man with no time to waste they got dressed and headed back downstairs.

What took you guys so long your food is getting cold co-co said. I had to slip into something more comfortable I had those tight ass clothes on all day and they were starting to cut my circulation off bit said. And what about you cuz co-co said, oh I was doing number two Vinnie said. Right tell me anything you two were doing the nasty weren't you co-co said.

Na'll I told you I was using the restroom I don't know why you think I'm lying to you cuz Vinnie said. What's up fill me in on the take I'm tired of being in the dark Duke said. Laughing, I'm hungry excuse me little bit said looking at co-co like she really wanted to tell her she just fucked the shit out of her little cousin.

Do you want me to fix you a plate Vinnie she continued, yeah thanks he said. Might as well make it candlelight and turn on some slow music co-co said laughing dat sounds like a good idea. Ya'll mind if I turn on the stereo Duke said no go right ahead and why don't you take your company with you why your at it little bit said.

Co-co didn't say a word she liked the idea of being with Duke anyway especially alone so they both went into the living room. Co-co found a comfortable spot on the sofa while Duke sat on the carpet in front of the stereo looking for something to put in. Duke you don't have to sit on the floor you can grab one of those chairs out the dinning room ta sit in while your looking for something ta play. All right what you wanna hear though?

It don't matter what ever you wanna listen to is fine with me. How about some T.I. he said na'll play some fifty-cent. All right. The music came on and every thing started to fall in place for Co-co she felt like dancing soon as the cd started to play. Duke just sat there rolling up some of his weed.

Let me fire that blunt up Co-co said looking at duke with a smirk like do you know I wanna fuck or what. When I'm finish you can lite it up if you want he said. Damn nigga what you been doing for the last year who ever dat bitch is got yo head fucked up you act like you really went for that drag ass story they sent me grow up and getta hard on she thought.

You know any new dances she said a couple but I mostly rap now, let me hear something then. Ok I sell dope and fuck count money and stuff preach for a livin when I'm smoking a blunt mmmm now the fuckin part yeah but the preachin part well he can keep that for his self. Now I have to make up a lie to try and stay on his good side she thought.

Damn, shit sound kinda raw Duke what's your rap name. I ain't got one yet but I'm workin on it, you really think I got what it takes he said? Yeah now come over here next to me so I can here exactly what you're saying. Duke got up out the chair and walked toward the sofa here you gotta liter. I thing so hand me my purse I believe its one in there, yeah here it is coco his her smile while liting the blunt with both hands like the wind was blowing inhaling then coughing as her eyes started to water.

She looked into Dukes eyes what's the matter with you nigga you can't rap it that's what you thinking I'm just trying to past time until they get through eatin then you can take yo ass in there and help Vinnie cook so I can sneak outside and give you two flat tires. Yo ass can't leave until I tell you. You can nigga she thought.

Duke continued to rap while co-co sat there watchin and smoking the weed. Rap after rap played while co-co continued to act like he was really impressing her before Vinnie finally called him in to the kitchen.

Hey we gotta whole brick here to cook so you know it's gonna take a minute to get finish I'll cook half then you can cook the other half he said. All right dats cool go for what you know Duke said. Little bit had already put a pot of water on the stove to boil while Vinnie rambled through the cabinets to find a mason jar.

He started pouring cocaine in the jar until it was almost halfway full then sat it directly in the middle of the pot. This shouldn't take long he thought as he poured water into the jar with a teaspoon. The soda he though I almost forgot rushing to the refrigerator to grab a box just in time. He started spooning soda in the jar as the coke started to bubble then take a liquid form.

Diss shit look like some good crack he said holding the jar high above his head. Yeah dat shit white as fuck Duke said. And it's ready Vinnie said putting the jar under some cold water. Instantly the liquid turned solid and Vinnie knew it was done he took the rock to the table and set it on a plate he took out earlier to let dry while he continued to cook.

The girls sat in the living room talking while the guys finished cooking. Girl you know your cousin can fuck his ass off little bit said. I knew you and him were up to something to much time had passed co-co said. What you and Duke do kiss and shit little bit said. Hell naw dat nigga act like he in a dream world the whole time Ya'll was upstairs.

He ain't done nothing but talk about his new car, all girls its so fast I can't wait to take you for a spin if he was to wreck it he'd probably have a fit Co-co said. Mmmm sounds like you're a little moody maybe some goose a set you right little bit said. Grey Goose where now that's all a I need is ta get drunk so I can really act a fool co-co said.

Huh little bit said handing her the keys its in the back of the truck under some clothes grab the gym bag to while your at it she said. Co-co sprung to her feet remembering what she had thought earlier she wanted so bad for Duke to spend the night but really didn't know how she would take it if he was to turn her down so she grabbed the keys from little bit then walked toward the kitchen excuse me guys I have to get something real quick.

Grabbing a corkscrew remover from the drawer what's that for Duke said? Little bit gotta bottle in the truck she said leaving out the kitchen. Hey girl save me some he hollered as co-co jumped down three steps to the landing in front of the side door quickly turning anything in her path upside down as she managed to get the door open leading to the drive way.

She ran down the side of the house straight to Duke's car and took a real hard swing at his back tire with the cork screw opener in hand it was a sharp popping noise then the pressure from the air inside the tire started to release from the hole making a sound like a tea kettle right before it started to whistle she then went to the other side of the car and did the same to the front tire laughing to herself.

She thought of how upset he was going to be when he found out she then took the corkscrew opener and shoved it in her back pocket as she approached Lil-Bits S.U.V. Now how can I do this she thought Lil-Bit uh probably ask me for the keys soon as I get back in the house and then my whole plan will be ruined. I don't wanna tell her cuz then she might tell Vinnie and I no he'll eventually tell Duke then he'll never speak to me again. That's all I need is two niggas in one day so I'm uh play it bye ear see what happens she thought before she stepped back in the door.

The guys were still in the kitchen but Lil-Bit had went upstairs to the bedroom she wanted to get some relaxation plus she really didn't like the smell of cocaine cooking. Co-Co weaved her way threw the kitchen to the cabinet ignoring what the guys were doing you want something to drink? She said setting the glasses on the counter s she went to the fridge to get some ice. Yeah Vinnie said. Co-Co poured every one a shot then left the kitchen she wondered threw the dining room admiring the beautiful pitchers on the walls. Where is Lil-Bit she thought standing in the middle of the living room floor. Lil Bit where you at where Lil-Bit at yall? I'm up here she said. Girl what you using the bathroom Co-Co said. Naw come on up here she said. Co-Co walked up the stairs threw the hall and in the bedroom to see Lil-Bt stretched out in the middle of the bed.

Girl what you doing she said? Its getting kinda late you know and I still have to get up early tomorrow and take care of some business plus go see face to Lil-Bit said. Yeah you right here's your drink what you got on the tube she said. Oh girl I don't know what this shit is I just turned it on Lil-Bit said. Well I'm going to let you get some rest you look like you need it but if you need anything just holler down stairs I'll be in the living room chilling.

Ok Lil-Bit said and can you tell Vinnie to come here when he's finish. Yeah girl Co-Co said as she walked out the door. It don't look like she's going anywhere else tonight o I guess Dukes really stuck here with me she thought now I can get him to do what ever I want him to do to me after I finish getting him drunk.

Co-co went to the kitchen to tell Vinnie what little bit had said he had already finished his cooking so he headed upstairs. Duke was just about finished when co-co came to tell Vinnie to go see what little bit wanted and was nagging her to make him another drink she sat at the table scoping him out why she made him another drink giving him a sarcastic look every time he glanced back to see if she had finished pouring his liquor.

Co-co walked toward the stove with the glass of liquor in her hand brushing her body against his as she eased around him to set the glass on the counter. Take your time she said rubbing her hand across his back then quickly raising the glass of liquor to his chest inquiring him to take a drink he reached for the glass swallowing the shot in one gulp then handed the empty glass back to her thanks, I needed that he said.

Co-co took the glass and turned back walking toward the table. Duke smacked her across the ass before she barely gotta chance to take one step back across the floor, she turned around looking at him with tears in her eyes. That hurt Duke she said he just stood there for a second then reached out and grabbed her cunt and started massaging it with his hand.

I'm sorry how can I make it up to you he said? I don't know let me think of something she said unbuttoning her pants. Duke watched as she back peddled to the table and started pouring drinks she quickly returned to his side with the glasses and her pants zipper half way down exposing her panties and thin pubic hairs.

First lets have a toast for old time sake then you can take me in the living room and rap to me with your shirt off you know how I love a man wit big muscles. Duke took his drink leaving Co-co with one hand free to wonder all over his body she quickly grabbed his cock cuffing it as she buried her face in his chest.

They both casually sipped on their drinks and continued to fondle and kiss each other before turning the stove off and retiring back to the living room. Co-co's face had started to swell from the passionate moods she was experiencing during this time and it started to show in the cresses under her eyes.

Before she had a chance to realize what was happening Duke was standing over her as she sat on the couch worker her fingers like a grandmother crocheting knitting a cover for the winter in December to get his pants undone. She then took him into her warm mouth causing his body to suddenly shake and fold over her head as it moved back and forth like a jackhammer beating on cement.

He quickly covered her ears with the palms of his hands pulling himself out then slowly pushing himself back in he continued to do this for a short while until she needed air. As this went on she began to pull on his growing penis slowly rubbing it back and forth in her hand as she tried to catch her breath.

Co-co had made her mind up Duke would be her sex toy for the time being and if things went the way she had planned he would be there for her tomorrow while little bit went to take care of her business. Duke let me take off my clothes for you so we can finish what we started it'll only take a second. She then stood up in front of Duke and slowly kissed him on his bottom lip before walking across the floor cutting the light off leaving very low visibility as she undressed her body was a shadow before Dukes eyes adjusted to the darkness revealing the beauty her clothing had so long hid.

Their bodies collided as they held each other passionately kissing and breathing like two wild animals lusting under the moon light this went on for a hour or so before Co-co and Duke both fell asleep inside each others arms.

The next morning little bit woke up at seven am. She threw Tricks pajama bottoms on and a t-shirt slipped on her shoes and was out the door her first stop was the super K-mart. She needed clean clothes to wear since going back to Barrowhead was out of the question once she finished shopping she headed straight for the bank she knew if she was planning on keeping Tricks empire going first she would have to find out what was going on with the payments and upkeep.

Good morning Mrs. Blackstreet little bit said to the bank teller, might I speak with your manager. Yes may I have your name the teller said? Yavette Robinson little bit said. Thank you, have a seat in the lobby and she'll be right with you. Ms. Robinson the teller said. Good morning Ms. Robinson I'm Mrs. Atchason the bank manager would you like to step into my office so we can discuss your business matter a little further she said. Yes little bit said.

The ladies walked through the lobby and into an office Mrs. Atchason took a seat behind her desk you may have a seat Ms. Robinson. Little bit did so now what seems to be the problem today the lady said. My fiancé just passed the day before yesterday and I need to know how many of his business assets and mortgage accounts he has that I'm co-owner of.

Ok what is his name Mrs. Atchason said. David Wakefield little bit said. Great I'll just punch his name in the computer and see what we have. Hmmm alright it seems that you are co-owner of ten houses, a barber ship, a beauty salon, and four vehicles, now the houses and the businesses are paid for but the vehicles are under a lease agreement in other words you now have to pay thirty two hundred dollars a month plus fifteen hundred dollars in land taxes and trash removal every three months for the ten houses and two business. Mrs. Atchason said.

I don't understand David told me that he had twenty thousand dollars in bills to pay every month before he died little bit said. There is some trueness to what he was telling you. You see every business and home he has is not paid for there for he has to pay the bank fifteen thousand dollars by the end of this month or he will fall behind on eight other houses three businesses and two vehicles which wouldn't be hard for you to pay if you could come up with the money Mrs. Atchason said.

But how would I become owner of the rest of his assets without my name being on the lease agreement little bit said. Ms. Robinson since your name is the only other one that shows up on some of the property the courts would have to take that into account before foreclosing the property and assets he owns meaning you would more than likely become full owner of everything. Mrs. Atchason said.

When would we be able to set up a court dat to handle this matter little bit said. Well it shouldn't take more than a couple days except I need a death certificate and some form of identification from you Mrs. Atchason said. I'll have to get a death certificate from the coroners office but I do have a State I.D. and drivers license some where around here little bit said digging through her purse.

Oh here it is, I'll just go ad make a copy and then bring this right back to you Ms. Robinson she said walking out the office. Little bit got on her ell phone and called to make funeral arrangement for the day after tomorrow while Mrs. Atchason was out making copies.

Ok Ms. Robinson here's your drivers license and also a copy of every property and asset you and Mr. Wakefield own, oh and by the way he has a banking and checking account that will be turned over to you after the courts are finished collecting their taxes if you can have that death certificate back to me by today then I can probably have this matter settled by the end of this week she said.

Fine little bit said taking a business card with her number on it I'll call you this afternoon to let you know if I was able to get the certificate and thanks for everything Mrs. Atchason she said and rushed out the office.

Damn dats exactly what I needed to hear now if I could hurry up and get to the coroners office and pick up the paper work then go pay the funeral home I could shower and get dressed in time to make it back to the bank she thought weaving in and outta traffic and speeding through lights just in time before they turned red.

Shit little bit said I forgot to get gas last night looking at the needle sitting behind E. If it wasn't for the auto gas mileage beeping I woulda probably sat at a light and ran out she thought looking for the nearest gas station in eyesight. Lucky ass bitch she thought spotting a pump and snack just down the street she pulled in the pump and snack coasting around the parking lot looking for a free pump as the dual exhaust rumbles off the cement walls of the building.

When all of a sudden gun shots started to rang out little bit quickly looked around to see where the shots were coming from when she seen a man standing inside the gas station ordering the cashier to give up the money she watched in utter disbelief. As the man put the gun to the cashiers head and pulled the trigger she fell to the floor as the man jumped over the counter banging the register with the butt of his gun he quickly scooped the cash up and ran out the station.

Oh my god little bit said when she realized tat it was Gutta she ducked down in the seat as he jumped in his car and smashed out. Her body started to shake and tears started to fall from her eyes she still managed to get gas before she left and quickly called 911 on her way to the coroners office.

Yes I'd like to report a murder at the pump and snack on Main Street she said. Ok what happened the operator said. I pulled up to get gas when all of a sudden I heard gunshots she said then what happened the operator said. A man came running out the building with a gun in his hand she said. Did you get a good look at him the operator said?

Yes I knew him from my projects she said. What projects the operator said. Barrowhead she said. Do you know his name the operator said? No I just know they call him Gutta she said. Your name the operator said?

Huh she said. What is your name the operator said. Yavette Robinson she said. Ok thank you very much and please stay on the line.

Little bit stayed on the line long enough for the operator to dispatch the police and ambulance to the scene. Ok where are you now mam the operator said? On my way to the coroner's office she said. Well I guess there's not too much more you can do for us at this time but I can get in touch with you at this umber for a full description of the suspect the operator said? Yes mam little bit said. Ok thank you and have a nice day the operator said, hanging up the phone.

Later at the coroner's office, hello young lady how may I help you the older man behind the desk said. I need a copy of my late fiancé's death certificate she said, and what is his name the man said. David Wakefield she said. Just one minute let me run the computer and have the printer print you a copy up. Looks like your still in your night clothes young lady musta had a kinda rough night huh he said punching buttons on the keyboard looking at her then back at the computer.

Yeah I guess you could say dat, I was up rather late she implied. It must be in the weather or something because I can't do it I'm to old in order for me to get up this early I have to lay down at about six just so I can make it through the whole day without falling asleep at my desk he said laughing.

You have to consider your age for a fella old as you it really doesn't seem out the ordinary for you to have to get so much rest I mean eight hours is a long time to be staying up she said. Your absolutely right mam thanks for the advice here's your certificate and have a nice day he said. Thanks and I enjoyed your conversation to hope you can find something for your sleep disorder she said. Waving as she walked out the door.

Hey! Hey! Wake up man Duke said. Still half sleep Vinnie turned over in the bed what is it man he said. Man somebody flattened my tires last night now we gonna have to wait till little bit get back so she can take me to get some new ones Duke said. Damn we might be stuck here all day and shit Vinnie said. Fuck dat I'm bout to call a tow truck and have it towed to the shop then she can just take us to pick it up when she gets back Duke said.

Man you thought about who might of did it I mean Treese dim ain't no you thing Vinnie said. Look cuz I don't know right now I gotta get going I got shit ta do today like sell all dat shit yo girl gave us plus check up on baby girl. I know she ain't tripping but man my family can't function without me cuz you dig Duke said with a sarcastic smirk on his face as he continued to talk picking up the phone what's up wit yo girl though you gonna tell me about it or what he said dialing the tow company.

Hold up! Yeah hello is this the 24 hour tow truck company? A grizzly voice spoke through the line, yeah this is the 24 hour tow hay my car is stuck how soon can you come and pick it up and run it to the shop for me? Bout a half and hour, alright I a be here Duke said hanging up the phone go head you want to the restroom man don't tell me you hit it in the tub on some gansta shit.

Naw she start callin me and shit I guess she ain't trust me or something anyway when I got to the door she all bent over lookin for her panties and shit. Was the ass fat? Hell yeah plus she got some nice titty's man I don't remember what happened all I know is I end up beatin da pussy up on the dresser for a couple of minutes. I nutted so quick cuz da pussy was so wet dats when co-co start tryin ta tease but it ain't work.

Yeah ma nigga got right on the exquisite side duke said laughing continuing ta tease so can she fuck? Hell yeah. Damn sound like a winner ta me. What ya'll in here laughing about Co-co said busting in the room. Damn you noisy as fuck girl. I couldn't help ta over hear all that damn laughing you two was up here doing she said.

Old Times they said, Old times my ass ya'll niggas talking bout what happened last night ain't ya'll. I thought you was tired go back to sleep Duke said. I was but I ain't no more ya'll hungry? Yeah what you plan on cookin girl? Don't worry about it leaving out the room just have ya'll asses up when it's done!

Little bit thought about Trick leaving the funereal home, damn Trick why you have to go and get kilt on uh bitch? I wish you were here to witness Gutta and Eleit your suppose ta be niggas rob and rape me now everybody wanna kill somebody instead of havin the police do there own damn job I don't need nobody to protect me I can handle myself just fine she continued this the rest of the way back to the house.

She noticed a tow truck pulling Duke's car away as she pulled in the drive mmmm what's this about rushing into the house Duke do you know someone's towing your car? Yeah someone flattened my tires last night you think you you'll have time to take me to pick it up in a couple hours? I have to get dressed and run back to the bank but after that I'll be free for the rest of the day you hungry Vinnie said yeah! Well you can finish my plate I really don't have a big appetite this morning.

Is everything ok co-co said? Yeah I'll tell you about it later I have to hurry up and get dressed so I can make it back to the bank. Are you gonna eat he said? Yeah just put it in the microwave for me ok. And since you're in such a good mood I need you to help me straighten up upstairs since you're in such a giving mood this morning she said kissing his lips. No problem.

They quickly disappeared leaving Co-co and Duke to themselves full of mischief and curiosity I bet you twenty dollars their going to make out in the shower Co-co said. No bet Duke said shaking the bottle of syrup why spend time thinking about what they doing when we haven't finished what you started last night.

I thought you were to drunk to remember any of that stuff I did to you last night. Really well that because I haven't had a chance to thank you just yet popping open the bottle of syrup it's been a long time since a woman has done things to me like that I think your joking I bet every chic you've slept with sucked you off at least once or twice.

Eyeing the syrup placing her hand over the open top so stop lying and tell me what you plan on doing with this syrup pushing the bottle against his chest. Well lets go to the shower in the basement so you can have our revenge without making a mess then I can really express my feelings in a more intimate setting without arousing anyone's attention. That way I'll be able to enjoy the things you plan on doing to me with that syrup grasping his hand leading him to the basement door.

Girl I have to go to the house and get in the shower all that business stuff has got me exhausted I really need a break how bout you? Little bit said. Right co-co said with a slight touch of sarcasm, what's with you little bit quickly responded I told you that Yo-yo thing is not important right now you'll have your day ok I promise. I know its just getting to me a little that's all I'll be fine. Hey after we get dressed how bout us two go and have a drink at the Hop Scotch down on fifth what'll you say it'll be fun little bit said. Ok I'm wit that I do need two stiff shots right about now how long you think you gonna be for you ready.

Oh about twenty minutes tops. Alright I'll roll up a couple blunts then fry some chicken by that time you should be ready huh. Yeah little bit said pushing her fist out to give Co-co dap for all the help and effort she been giving her the last couple days.

Nigga were you been all night, I called here two times last night and ain't nobody have a clue as to where you where you were now don't you think you got some explaining to do Treese said. I ain't got nothing to explain I was on the block all night hustling trying ta get my pockets right see there you go thinking you know it all. Ooo something just telling me to believe you but I checked all your usual spots and guess what hadn't nobody seen you yeah I did a little check really dick huntin cause ma stupid ass got drunk and wanted to fuck but you lying so where was you Treese said folding her arms across her chest.

Girl quit trippin I went down to Barrowhead ta kick it wit my cousin Co-co dats why you couldn't find me anyway I told you I had something ta do it ain't my fault you got drunk and forgot. So what if I told you I went down there too. Bitch quit lying you know you ain't took yo crazy ass to Barrowhead looking for me.

Why I gotta be a bitch all the time huh? Cause you is, always getting on my nerves and shit. I know baby but that's cuz I care about you. Well what ever it is you need to quit it because its aggravating and don't start trying ta kiss up because I ain't in the mood plus I got some shit ta take care of and fuckin ain't one of um so you might as well call you a cab and get ready to go home.

Where you going? Don't worry about it just be gone when I get out the shower. I ain't going anywhere I'm stayin here until you get back. Ok keep thinking dat and see how quick I fuck you up. Alright what ever fuck me up cuz I ain't movin. So you wanna be a smart ass huh well go on and sit there when the police het here they uh be happy to escort yo dumb ass outta here.

You gotta lotta nerves callin the police and you know I gotta warrant. Well you shouldn't of stole that shit out the mall den you wouldn't have that problem. Nigga fuck you mostly everything I steal be for your black ass anyway I dare you to call em go ahead.

Naw I ain't gonna call em I was just trying to scare you off you can chill but I don't know why you think you runnin shit around here. Treese didn't say another word she just rolled her eyes then sat down on the bed. She picked up the phone and started dialing his number.

Hello is he there? He is sleepin right now may I ask who's calling? Yo-yo oh how are you doing? Alright, well he told me to tell you if you called to call him back a little later. Ok tell him to call me when he wakes up. Ok I'll be sure to tell him. Thanks. She hung up the phone and turned back towards Treese.

He knew he had to get his le straight with Duke before Treese talked to her. You look like you've been up all night crying, I have worrying about yo ass. He cut his eyes quickly trying to think of something. Trees look I'm sorry for calling you out your name but I have a lot on my mind right now but don't think I've forgot about you I know you love me more than anything in the world and you know I feel the same way about you.

Right now I need you the most you've been the only one in my corner for a long time asd I feel like you should trust me as much as I trust you. Busy trying to think of something else to tell Treese while he figured while he figured out what he was going to do about this situation in front of him, when it all came clear.

Treese can you do me a favor while I'm gone? What now. I need you to hold on to this sack, try and make dollar for dollar not shorts you think you can do that for me? Yeah I guess, when you comin back though? I'm not sure could be tonight or maybe even tomorrow but if it's any problem I'll pay you for your troubles.

Baby you don't have to pay me I'm your bitch but you could be nice and give your bitch some of dat dick before you leave. Treese slowly put her finger to the corner of her mouth then licked her lips and waved her finger for him to come over to the bed where she was. He just stood there looking at her with a smirk on his face. You silly, at least let me get in the shower first. Treese rolled her eyes again. Ok but hurry up I don't wanna here no excurses either when you get out like you tired cuz I'm a wait right here. Alright I'm a only be a minute he grabbed his boxers and deodorant and left for the bathroom.

Co-Co! Little bit hollered from her room is the chicken ready yet? Just about. Hey I want a thigh and a leg, did you find the hot sauce? Yeah Co-co hollered back upstairs. Shit co0co thought to herself dat damn girl want hot sauce on everything she eat I'm a be sure to remind her to stop at the store so we can load up on it for she have a fit.

I see you've finally woke up I thought you would sleep until tomorrow the way you were snoring over there . . . Mom you always seem to bring out the best in a bad situation, what the doctors say. You'll be fine and those girls been callin all day asking about you but every time they would call . . . Face quickly cut in wait a minute I didn't mean to cut you off but what girls? You know little bit Tricks girlfriend well widow or whatever you young people call it and the . . .

Face cut her off again Co-co you mean to tell me they've been calling up here to see about me how'd they find out . . . I'm not sure I forgot how they had found out but they were sure up here soon as they heard about it . . . Hell naw mom I can't believe they even came. What you mean you know how women is. now tell me how are they . . . Mom I ain't mean it like that.

Well how do you mean it? You know they young and fast in just surprised they even had time to stop did they leave a number? Yeah you want me to call them? Yeah! Alright calm down though I don't want you to go back into a coma. She picked up the telephone and started dialing little bits number.

Girl yo phone ringing you want me to answer it co-co said? Yeah, Hello Hello little bit? No this is Co-co oh I must have dialed the wrong number. No this is little bits phone may I ask who I'm speaking to. This is Face's mother, oh how is he?

Well he's doing much better. Did he wake up yet? As a matter a fact yes and he wants to speak with you guys. He's kinda excited to talk to you two but you know the doctors said to try and keep him calm so if it gets outta hand he'll have to talk to you two later, but here he is.

What up? You baby how you doin? I'm alright just a little sore. Well you know you need to get as much rest s possible so you can get back out here where you belong. I know I'm chilling though, I heard ya'll came up here to see me where little bit at? She upstairs. Little bit come get the phone its Face he wanna talk to you.

We a probably be up there to see you sometime today alright. Damn what she doing. Her ass up there getting dressed you want me to bring you some chicken up there. Who cooked it? Me nigga what you think I can't cook or something? Na'll I ain't say dat I was hopin it was home cooked anyway but yeah rush it a.s.a.p. A nigga hungry as hell.

You don't know if the doctors gonna let you eat outside food yet why you ordering stuff over the phone his mom said. I know mom I'm ordering it for you anyway. Hello what's up nigga you had a bitch scared for a minute. I'm so glad to hear your voice again. You need anything just let me know.

Damn girl you got on the phone and ain't stop talkin yet give a nigga a chance to at least say hi or something. Aw nigga please you sound good though to have just got shot up . . . Girl this a gorilla you talking to I could go home right now if it was up to me.

Nigga keep talking like that and I'm a have to tie you up in my backyard for protection. Hey bit you silly ass hell. I'm out with you nigga if you wasn't my dude's nigga I think I probably woulda hollered at yo crazy ass but I gotta put some lotion on so holla t Co-co . . . Alright girl hello, yeah what yall laughin about sound like you enjoying yoself.

What ever it was did I miss out on something? Naw we was just talking shit dats all what's up with dat business shit though? Oh I don't really know but I think she got everything under control. Yeah dats good I can't wait to get back out there to help her out. I know boo it shouldn't be to long now you a probably be out in a couple days back to your old self. Shit I hope so this bed uncomfortable as hell. I know you a be alright though, well I got your chicken all packed up and ready for you. Ok I'm a let you two go but don't leave me hanging alright, yeah nigga we uh be there Co-co hung up the phone.

Yo still gotta go back to that bank and get shit straight with them? Yeah soon as I find these bank receipts and holla at your cousin you know so where we going first? Well I ain't really sure cause I figured the bank will probably take at least another hour before they have all the paper work ready and I don't wanna get drunk before I go back so you got anything you wanna get out the way why we got time. No but we can take this chicken over to Face and his mom for it get cold. Alright lets go.

Niggas betta recognize bitches always try and lie but I'm a little nigga from the hood that make them realize Black rapped out loud to himself as he walked down the street. Hey little nigga what you doing roaming the streets all by yourself Yo-yo said from the passenger seat of the car slowly rolling down the street?

Minding my business what about you girly? I'm looking for little bit you seen her Black quickly grew suspicious. Little bit I ain't never heard of no little bit. Dats all right little nigga I a find her myself Yo-yo said as the car slowly started to gain speed. All right get at me though Black yelled. He was thinking to himself who was that bitch anyway what the fuck she think this is don't she know everybody in Barrowhead stick together dumb trick.

Maybe we should shoot down to Barrowhead and see if we can find Black I know he's probably scared ta death all alone you know he was the only one with Face when he got shot little bit said. Yeah your right we should hurry before whoever shot Face comes back and tries to shoot him if he's not going to be any trouble.

I don't think he'll be too bad. Yeah you right so are you going to pick hi up before you stop at the hospital? Of course he's probably wondering what's going on his self damn I almost missed the turn its going to be kinda hard recognizing him we don't even know what he has on or where he lives so kinda keep a eye out cause we don't need to be down here that lone as it is.

Bit look there he is. Where, over there in the 110 parking lot serving a fiend and look he doesn't even notice us sitting in this big ass truck I mean what if we were the cops his ass would be hit. I'm about to pull over there. Yeah but look I'm uh be out here all day trying ta blow this shit so when you done smoking that shit you coped just holler out the window and I a be right up.

Ok little homey give me about half and hour or so. Black turned and watched the cocky dark skinned man walk towards his apartment not noticing little bit and co-co in the truck right behind him. Little bit rolled her window down then began to speak hey little man can I get some of that money you out here making or what.

Black instantly turned to see where the pretty voice had came from still echoing threw his ears when he saw little bit hanging her head out the window nearly blinded from her gold teeth shining as they slowly chewed down on the bubble gum.

Black drew his forearm over his eyes dragging his voice as he spoke hey bay bay whats the occasion or is my popularity steady growing without my knowledge? No boy I don't think so get yo young ass in the truck we came to take you to see Face and chill with us that is if you gonna behave little man looking at little bit laughing.

Black quickly ran to the truck and jumped in the back seat to come face to face with little bit, you always flirting around with older women almost twice your age? Yeah and I'm trying to get some hands on experience when possible. You out the pocket Black and I, I didn't even notice it Co-co why didn't you tell me I had a hard on before I got in? I coulda co-co quickly cut in wait a minute don't even try to pull that little thing out in front of bit she don't wanna see that little mothafucka. Co-co, Little bit said he just talkin shit. Smiling yeah co-co I'm just talking shit Black said, why you tripping over spilled beans?

Ain't nobody tripping you know ya'll niggas round here ignorant and ain't got no proper up bringing outta life. Who, Who ain't have proper upbringing mam, yes mam please, no thanks you and I apologize where you think I learned all that cause it wasn't in between yo legs why you sittin up there trying ta act brand new for bit.

All right I'm sorry Black I was just fuckin with you crazy, Ya'll better quit before ya'll make me wreck little bit said as she fought for dear life to regain control of her emotions. All right we gone chill co-co put my UGK in. What number? Just let it ride, back front and back and side to side. Back front and back and side ta side back front and back and side ta side never let hoe ass niggas ride.

Dats my shit Black said with authority. So you a gee huh little man bit said? Naw I wouldn't say all that just a young nigga with a hell of a lot of hustle. Well at least you sound sincere in what you say if you keep talking like that I'm sure you'll come up shit maybe one day you'll have enough to buy this truck. Nah I don't think so what if I give you some work to get off for me you know maybe an ounce to start with?

Just ta see how you do? It sound good but when is this suppose ta be taking place. Today if you want. Ok I'm with it. All right when we come from the hospital I'll drop you off back in Barrowhead why me and co-co go to the club for a little while then we'll come back and pick you up and take you to my house and you can spend the night with us it'll be fun.

Yeah now that's what's happening a night with two lovely ladies and some dough. I wouldn't miss it for the world ya feel me. Yeah we feel you co-co said. Oh yeah little bit come ta think about it some chic came through earlier looking for you I think she said her name was Yo-yo but I told her ass I didn't know you and she got mad and sped off. Yeah what color was the ride? Tan.

Well if you happen to see her again don't break your code of silence cause she's bad news. Yeah-real bad news co-co said. We're here are you guys ready to go in? yeah they both said what is he on then suddenly changing his facial expression and tone of voice he quickly whispered out there goes the car I seen earlier today and there's that chic I was telling you about standing by the smoke pit blazing an L.

All right stay calm everyone I'm sure she's not stupid enough to try and start anything with security close by bit said. Yeah sure right after that show she put down at McDonalds I'm not to sure I think I'll take my gun with me just in case you never can be to sure with clowns like her and her crew you know.

Ok I'll go first it's me she wants anyway so I'm a give her what she's looking for bit opened the door and quickly slid out on to the pavement bending down to unbuckle her sandals then throwing them on the floor inside the truck before she shut the door. Black you stay in the truck Face's room number is 357 when you see me cross the street get out and walk to the entrance by your self and don't speak to me or bit we don't want them to know you know us ok co-co said.

Yeah I hear you loud and clear. What's up bitch you lookin for me how here I am bit said. Yo-yo's eyes quickly started to squint as her nose flared up by this time both of bits hands were balled up like two knots still closing in on yo-yo then two other girls appeared bedside yo-yo.

Wait a minute this is my fight I'll handle this bitch on my own time when bit landed a overhand left square above yo-yo's eye stung but not dazed yo-yo took one step back and started tow swing back at bit with her palms open scratching and kickings her as bit grabbed her hair and started to pound her fist in the side of her head continuously until yo-yo fell to one knee.

Bitch I told yo ass about fuckin with me once now I'm gone beat yo motherfuckin ass ho bare footed and all bit continued to heat yo-yo like she had stole something with security came out to brake thinks up. All right ladies that's enough break it up. Hold up what ya'll doing they tried to jump my girl and ya'll grabbin on her like she started it co-co said.

Quiet down young lady everything gonna be alright I'm just doing my job the officer said. Yeah bit said. So are you going to lock my friend here up co-co said? No, No one's going to the slammer, but don't let it happen again. Now mam are you, before the officer could finish getting his words out yo-yo stuck a knife so deep in the side of his stomach it caused him to grunt and fold over for a few seconds before he finally collapsed to the ground.

Blood leaked out his wound heavily as he tried grasping the hole with his hands. Now bitch I'm gonna cut you up just like I cut up your rookie cop friend here pointing her bloody knife at the man. No you ain't bitch unless you ready to eat some lead co-co said brandishing her pistol in hand.

Now back up real slow I wouldn't want to make a mistake and think you were trying to pull my hoe card dirty trick. Hey the cops are coming

Black screamed. Yo-yo and her two road dogs jumped in the car and tried to make a run for it when cop cars swarmed the emergency exit blocking all traffic coming in or going out. Freeze mothafuckas the heavy set black cop said. Driver get yo ass out the car NOW! Somebody get some help for that man and hurry up before he dies.

Finally in Faces room he asked us have we read the paper? Well have you read about Carlos? Carlos, yeah Carlos the leader of the Latino's somebody killed his ass in cold blood. So you sayin they think you had something to do with it? Naw they probably went around all the hoods and shot somebody you know how them portaricans is if one theirs dies and they can't find out who did it they just go around killing everybody.

Yeah so I guess we better lay low from them for now. See bitch dats what I mean every fuckin time we gotta lay low like some suckas fuck dim bulldaggas can't you see dim faggots don't give a fuck who they take out so why should we? Co-co just chill girl. Hell naw I say we go over their and let loose on some of them bitches.

It's cool co-co I'm a be all right but ya'll got stop tripping and let me finish, now it was a bitch from yo-yo's crew dead up in the house to and the cops think she killed Carlos because she was found with the same gun that fired the shot in Carlos's head. Hold up dats what dat bitch yo-yo was talkin about.

Yeah well what ever she was talkin about she ain't gone be able to do it for a long time. Why? Cause the dumb bitch just killed a security guard in the parking lot. Downstairs? Yeah right out side the fuckin hospital. She don't give a fuck she a be right at home with the rest of them dykes. Aw ya'll think ya'll can drop me off little man? Why?

Cause ya'll hoe's on hot ya'll got some a everybody in the city lookin for ya'll. I mean I'm still young I gotta lotta life ahead of me, I ain't ready ta die! Boy please as much shit as you talk everyday all day I know dat difference, just be playing dis shit serious though man.

Oh babe I'll drop you off ok I didn't mean to scare you, I didn't know it was gone happen like this. Man, come on quit trying ta run game on us. I know you ain't scared for real Black said? Naw but I ain't even got my piece on me and you know dats a no, no in a situation like this